Bo(
Ele

M000077815

# Succeeding with the Masters®
# & The Festival Collection®
# ETUDES with Technique

## About the Series

This series is designed to develop healthy, natural, and effective technique so that students can play beautifully as well as with virtuosity. Each book is divided into units, and each unit focuses on one technical concept. Technical concepts are introduced using imagery to help the student understand the gesture needed to produce the correct technique. Different imagery is used in each level of this series. Following the text and the imagery, two short technical exercises provide the student's first opportunity to play the technique. These exercises should be memorized so students can focus on the sound they produce while observing their playing mechanism in action. Several etudes then follow to reinforce each technical concept. In this way, students focus on one technique at a time, and the concept is reinforced through multiple etudes. This method allows the student to master the technique and make it a habit, providing the foundation for effective, natural, relaxed, and enjoyable performances of their repertoire.

The student should concentrate on looking at their hands and being aware of the feeling in their fingers and fingertips, hands, wrists, forearms, elbows, and upper arms so as to produce the correct gestures. In order to achieve a fluid and solid technique, students must always listen carefully to themselves and the sound they create.

This series is best used with the following publications:

*Etudes with Technique, Book 1 = The Festival Collection®, Book 1 = On Your Way to Succeeding with the Masters®*

*Etudes with Technique, Book 2 = The Festival Collection®, Book 2 = An Introduction to Succeeding with the Masters® = Succeeding with the Masters®, Volume One*

*Etudes with Technique, Book 3 = The Festival Collection®, Book 3 = Succeeding with the Masters®, Volume One*

*Etudes with Technique, Book 4 = The Festival Collection®, Book 4 = Succeeding with the Masters®, Volume One*

THE
F·J·H
MUSIC
COMPANY
I N C.
Frank J. Hackinson

Production: Frank J. Hackinson
Production Coordinators: Joyce Loke and Satish Bhakta
Cover Art Concept: Helen Marlais
Cover Design: Terpstra Design, San Francisco, CA
Illustration: Keith Criss, TradigitalWorks, Oakland, CA
Engraving: Tempo Music Press, Inc.
Printer: Tempo Music Press, Inc.

ISBN-13: 978-1-56939-759-6

# Etudes with Technique, Book 1

# Practice Tips

An etude is a composition designed to help students master an instrument, or practice a technique. For all the units in this series, practice in the following ways:

1. Read over the text and the imagery for each technical concept. Then practice the two short technical exercises. Memorizing these short patterns will keep you focused on two important goals: achieving the best sound; and observing what your fingers, hands, wrists, forearms, elbows, upper arms, and shoulders are doing!

2. There is a helpful practice strategy above each etude to guide you in practicing or interpreting each etude.

3. Look over the entire etude to discover its patterns and the main technical concept that the etude addresses.

4. Practice the etude as you would repertoire pieces—with attention to detail, in short sections, isolating trouble spots, and hands-separate practice.

5. Once you learn the etude, practice it at different tempos. Always listen for a beautiful sound in your playing.

6. Transpose the etudes to other keys—one step up, one step down, a fifth up, from major to minor, and from minor to major to expand your technique.

7. Not only your fingers move when playing the piano. This series guides you to learn the function of the wrists, forearms, elbows, and upper arms. Also remember to keep your shoulders low and wide, relaxed, and sit tall at the bench.

   **Reviewing units often is an excellent way to establish a strong technical foundation. You will find that by going back to a previous unit after a period of time, that unit will be much easier to play the second time and reviewing it will confirm your technical mastery!**

# Etudes with Technique, Book 1

FJH2025

# UNIT 1 - FIVE-FINGER PATTERNS

**Five-Finger Patterns** are so important to all piano playing that you definitely want them to feel "natural!" Imagine that your fingers are like the legs of this baby t-rex and that you "walk" them from one to the next. Remember that just like you, he never has two feet down when walking, but lets the weight rest on the leg that is down. So when you play, roll the weight from one finger to the next, letting the finger that lifts come off the key at the same time as the next finger goes down. Keep your fingers curved, just as you keep your knees slightly bent to cushion your steps. Try "walking" your fingers on your leg so you can feel the weight of your arm resting on them.

Helen Marlais

Continue playing up the scale (DM, EM, FM …)

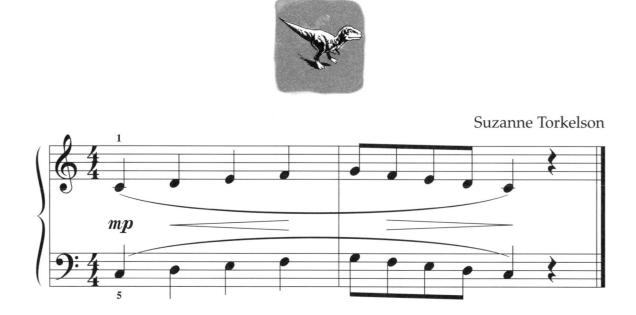

Suzanne Torkelson

Continue playing up the scale (DM, EM, FM …)

# ETUDE

## *(Opus 101, No. 15)*

• Before playing, play the piece silently on top of the keys.

Ferdinand Beyer
(1803-1863)

Transpose to: GM _____

DM _____

# Etude

### *(Opus 70, No. 10)*

• Plan the tempo before beginning to make sure you can play the
  second half of the piece at the same speed as the first half.

Hermann Berens
(1826-1880)

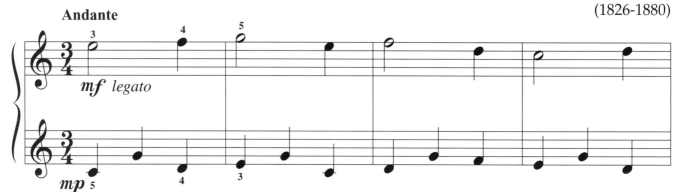

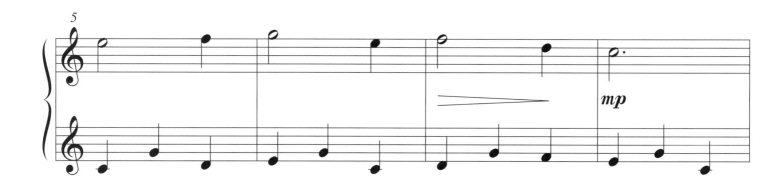

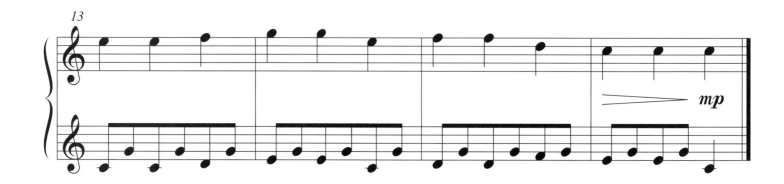

Transpose to: DM _____

# WOODLAND ELVES

- To help your fingers play evenly, roll the hand
  in the direction of the notes.

Valerie Roth Roubos
(1955-    )

*a tempo*
*8ᵛᵃ both hands until the end*

FJH2025

# ETUDE

*(Opus 823, No. 12)*

• Block the left-hand intervals first by playing all the notes of each measure
  at the same time. When playing the repeated notes, play on your fingertips.

Carl Czerny
(1791-1857)

* These notes are editorial and have been changed for consistency.

Transpose to: CM _____

# THE GREAT GATE OF KAZAN

• To create a full tone, support each finger by feeling the weight from
your arm directly behind each finger as you play from note to note.

Timothy Brown
(1959-   )

FJH2025

# Unit 2 - Staccato

Sometimes we want to make short, crisp sounds on the piano, so we use our fingers much like the hopping of this kangaroo. A kangaroo springs into the air by pushing off with its legs. Try this by starting with your fingertip on your leg and push off with a quick spring of your hand. Notice that neither the kangaroo nor you can push off without starting on the ground, or in your case, the keys. Let your fingertip come right back down, ready to spring again! You should hear crisp, short *staccato* tones, perfect for the playful or energetic melodies you are learning.

Suzanne Torkelson

Helen Marlais

Transpose to:  CM _____        Other Keys: ____ _____

DM _____                          ____ _____

AM _____

# ETUDE

## *(Opus 82, No. 19)*

• While playing, listen for the softer dynamic level of the *staccato* thirds.

Cornelius Gurlitt
(1820-1901)

# ALLEGRO

### from *24 Short and Easy Pieces, Opus 1*

• Play the *staccato* notes lightly. When playing with your thumb,
  play on the outside tip of this finger.

Alexander Reinagle
(1756-1809)

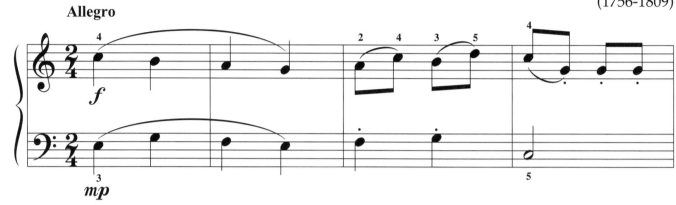

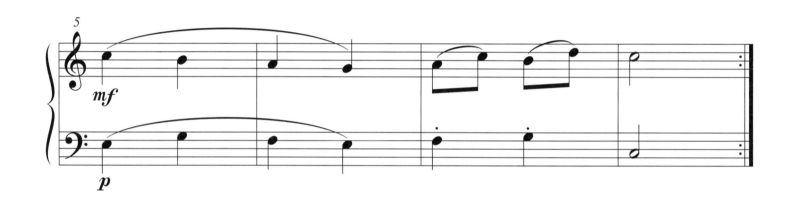

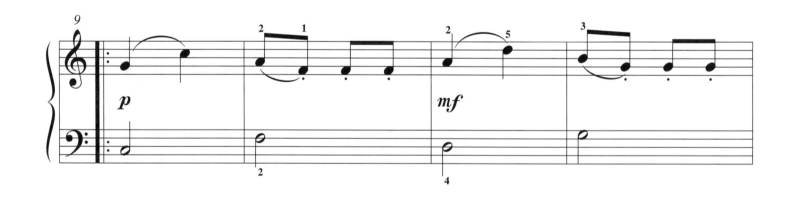

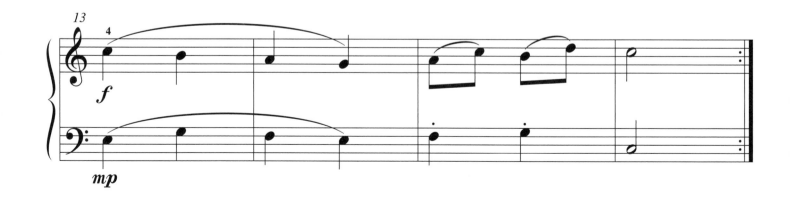

# Etude

### from *24 Five-Finger Exercises, Opus 777, No. 3*

• Listen for smooth five-finger patterns with a *staccato* bass pattern.

Carl Czerny
(1791-1857)

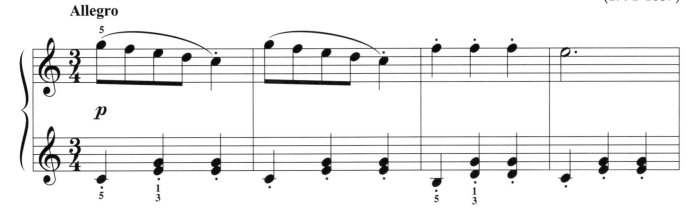

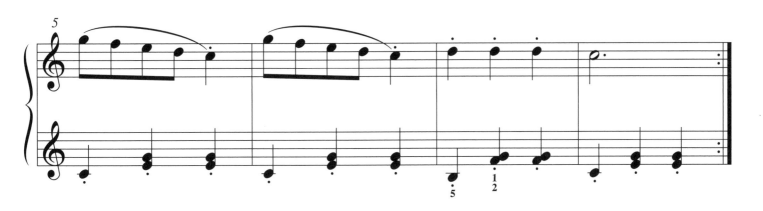

Transpose to: DM _____

FJH2025

# Stop at Nothing

- Listen carefully when playing the three-note slurs so that the first note is louder than the last note.

Timothy Brown
(1959-    )

# ETUDE

### (Opus 823, No. 11)

• Listen for the first note of each three-note slur to be the loudest
and for the staccato notes to be more quiet.

Carl Czerny
(1791-1857)

# UNIT 3 - LEGATO

Sometimes we want to make smooth, flowing sounds at the piano, so we make sure that a finger remains on the key at all times. Just like the "walking" of your five-finger patterns, you rest your arm on a finger, then move your weight to a new finger while letting the previous one lift out of the key. Notice that you feel a smooth glide of your arm from one note to the next, much like the gliding of our slippery snake. Keep those gentle curves in your fingers, just as you see in the snake. You will hear smooth, rich tones on the piano, perfect for the singing melodies you are learning.

Suzanne Torkelson

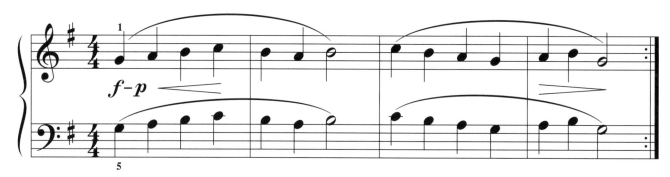

Transpose to: CM _____

DM _____

FM _____

AM _____

Helen Marlais

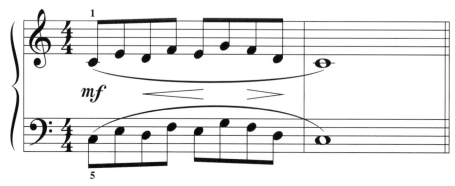

Continue playing up the scale (DM, EM, FM …)

# ETUDE

## *(Opus 101, No. 39)*

• Listen for the balance between the hands and keep the left-hand
  thumb touching the D for a soft repeated tone.

Ferdinand Beyer
(1803-1863)

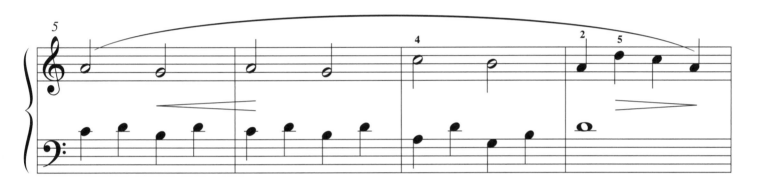

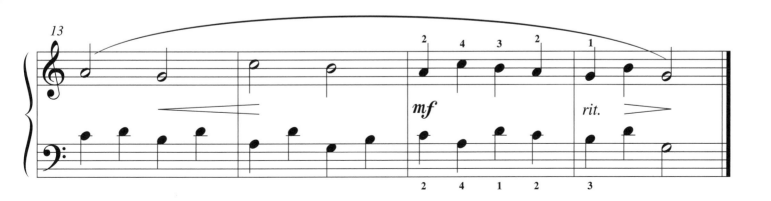

# ETUDE

## *(Opus 190, No. 16)*

• Before playing, block (play together) the left-hand notes to form triads.
  Then add the right hand. When comfortably blocked, play as written.

Louis Köhler
(1820-1886)

# ICE CRYSTALS

• Roll the left hand from side to side for a *legato* sound.

Valerie Roth Roubos
(1955-    )

**Con moto** (♩ = ca. 160-176)

*press pedal down*

*poco rit.*

*a tempo*

*rit.*

*pp*

\*Pick up your thumb to prepare the D in the next measure.

FJH2025

22

# ETUDE

*(Opus 190, No. 22)*

- Listen for an expressively shaped melody in the left hand.

Louis Köhler
(1820-1886)

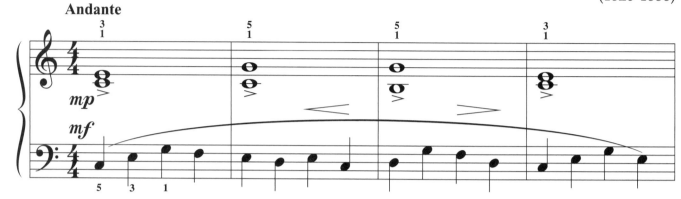

Transpose to: GM _____

# ETUDE

- When playing each quarter note, prepare your finger silently over the next key.

François Couperin
(1668-1733)

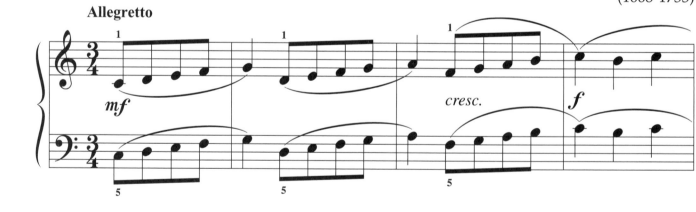

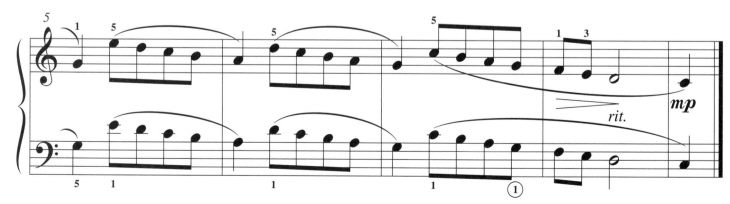

Transpose to: DM _____

# UNIT 4 - TWO-NOTE SLURS

One of the most important gestures you will learn when playing the piano is the "drop-lift" of a slur. Imagine that you are a baby kitten landing gently on the ground, then being picked up at the neck by your mother. As you roll your wrist forward and up, let your fingers hang loosely from the wrist, just as the kitten hangs in the air. When you land on the keys again, think of how the kitten lands gently on its paws for a cushioned landing. You will hear full tones on the drop landing, followed by softer tones on the roll off, perfect for tapering dynamics at the ends of phrases and giving your melodies beautiful expression.

Helen Marlais

Transpose to: GM _____

Suzanne Torkelson

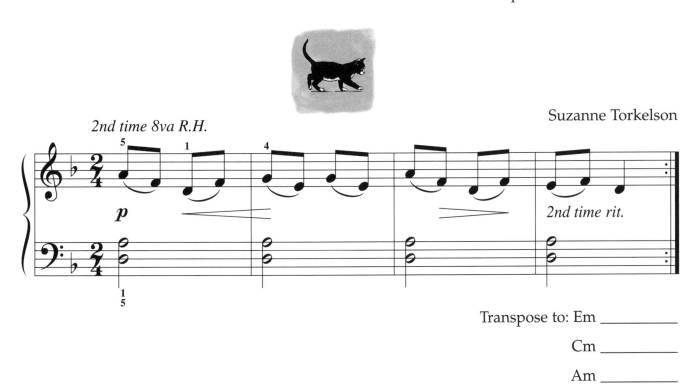

Transpose to: Em _____

Cm _____

Am _____

# ETUDE

## (Opus 117, No. 10)

• Move your wrists to connect the notes, and roll forward (away from your body and towards the fallboard) to play the left-hand thumb.

Cornelius Gurlitt
(1820-1901)

# Der Dudelsack

*(Opus 95, No. 1)*

• Practice the right hand until all the articulations are correct.
  Roll the hand from side to side in order to transfer the weight
  from finger to finger. Then add the left hand.

Heinrich Kaspar Schmid
(1874-1953)

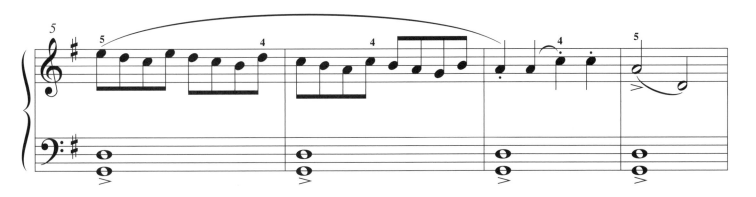

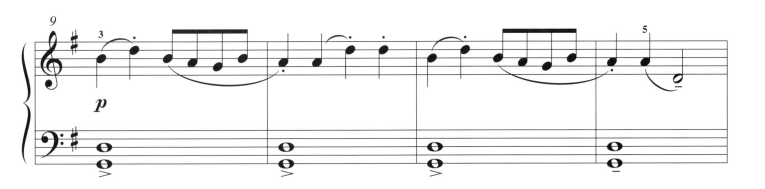

# Two by Two

• Before starting, silently block the positions of the right hand.
  Then block the left hand on the third line.

Robert Schultz
(1948-    )

**Allegro** (♩ = 168)

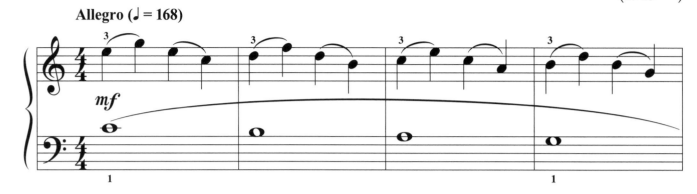

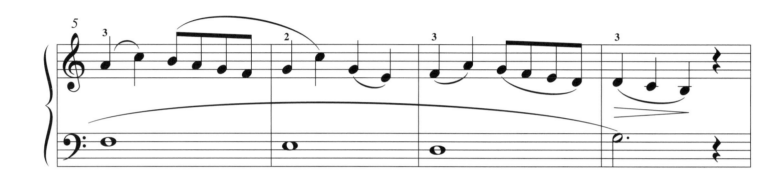

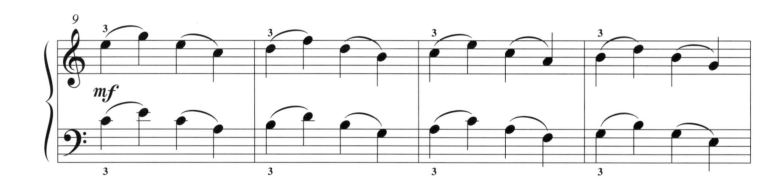

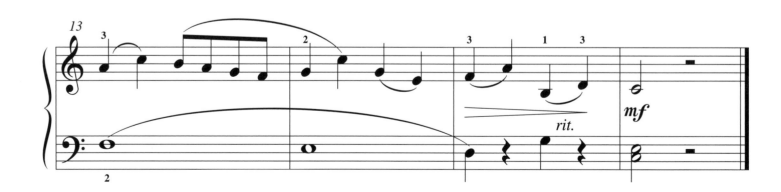

# Unit 5 - Two-Part Counterpoint

The next part of a "natural technique" is the ability to play hands independently of each other. Think of two tropical fish, similar in how they look, but one swims higher in the water or slightly ahead of the other one. When playing the piano, we often need to make similar sounds, yet with one hand taking the lead, either in timing or in dynamics. Try playing hands together, but playing one *forte* while the other *piano*. When you can do that, switch hands! You will hear a full tone in one hand, accompanied by softer tones in the other, perfect for helping your listener focus on the all-important melodies you are creating.

There are 2 kinds of counterpoint:

## "Imitative" Counterpoint

(Described above as two tropical fish.)

Helen Marlais

Transpose to: DM _____

## "Mirror" Counterpoint

(For every important note in the right hand, there is an equally important note in the left hand.)

Suzanne Torkelson

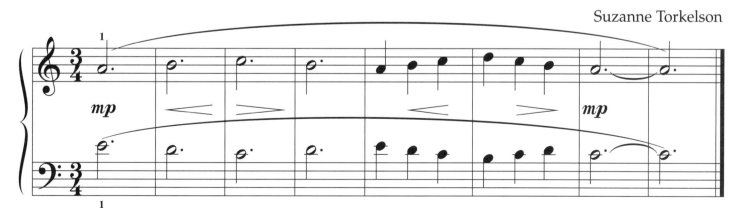

Transpose to: Dm _____

Gm _____

FJH2025

# ETUDE

*(Opus 117, No. 4)*

• Study the music–play the piece silently on top of the keys before playing
on the keys. When are the two lines parallel? When are they contrary?

Cornelius Gurlitt
(1820-1901)

**Con moto**

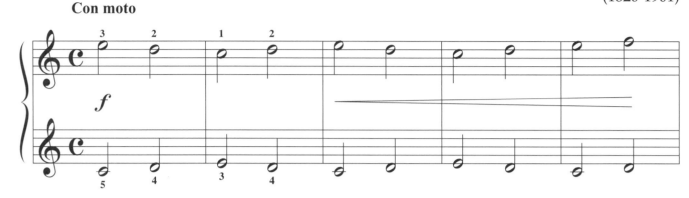

Transpose to: GM _____

# CANON NO. 15

from *200 Canons, Opus 14*

• Before playing, tap the piece hands together while counting aloud.

Konrad Max Kunz
(1812-1875)

**Deliberately**

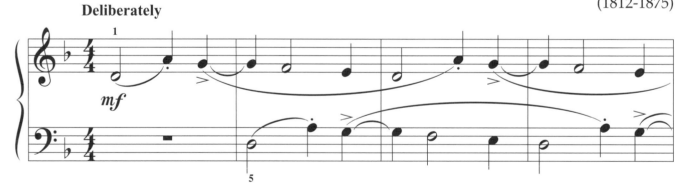

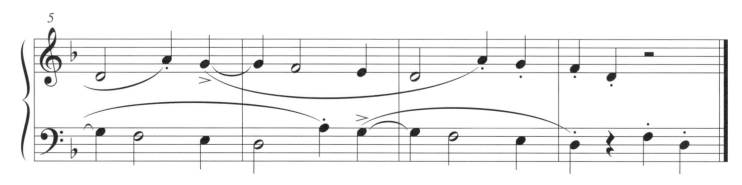

Transpose to: Cm _____

# STUDY IN CONTRARY MOTION

- Before playing, circle the only place where the hands do *not* play with the same fingers.

Johann Friedrich Reichardt
(1752-1814)

# DUO

- Count while you play in order to focus on the two equal parts at once.

Tomás de Santa Maria
(c.1515-1570)

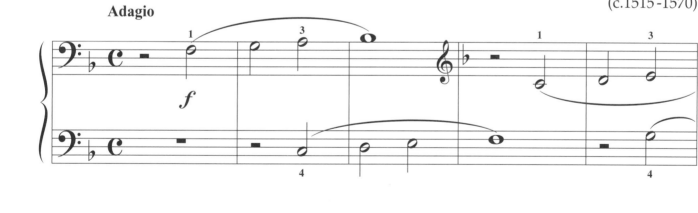

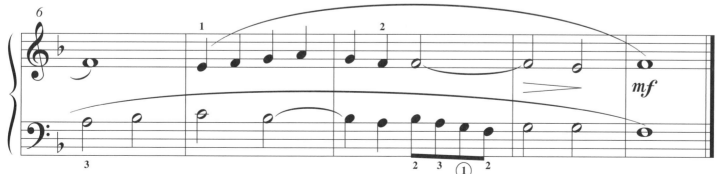

# ETUDE

## (Opus 82, No. 17)

• Make each and every note beautiful to your ears
  by shaping each phrase.

Cornelius Gurlitt
(1820-1901)

# UNIT 6 - HARMONIC INTERVALS

The last "natural technique" of this book is the technique of interval playing. On the piano, you can either play two keys at the same time, like the back legs of this giraffe, or play them one after the other, like his front legs. The distance between the notes is called an interval, which is just another word for space. When you play them at the same time, they are called "harmonic intervals," and when you play them separately, they are called "melodic intervals." Try playing harmonic or melodic intervals as a friend calls them out. Harmonic intervals are perfect for accompanying melodies, and melodic intervals are perfect for building melodies.

Helen Marlais

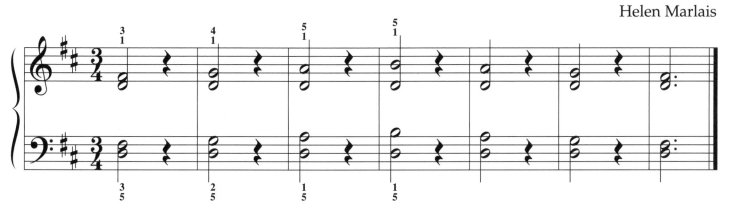

How many keys can you transpose this to?

—— ——————

—— ——————

—— ——————

• Be sure to replay the repeated notes but make the other voice smooth.

Suzanne Torkelson

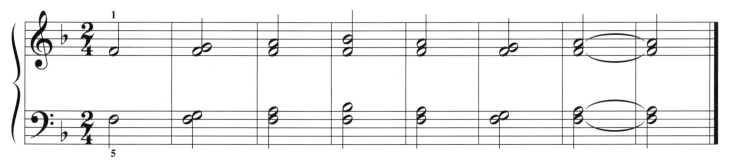

Transpose to: GM _____

EM _____

CM _____

FJH2025

# ETUDE

## *(Opus 101, No. 18)*

- Before playing, label all the harmonic intervals. The first
  one has been done for you. Listen for the repeated note of the
  harmonic intervals.

Ferdinand Beyer
(1803-1863)

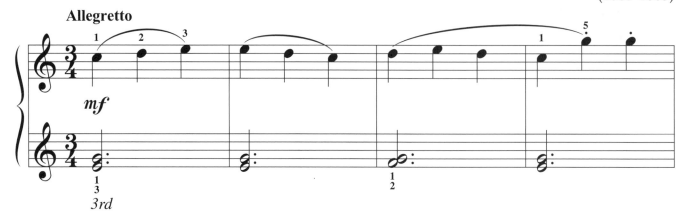

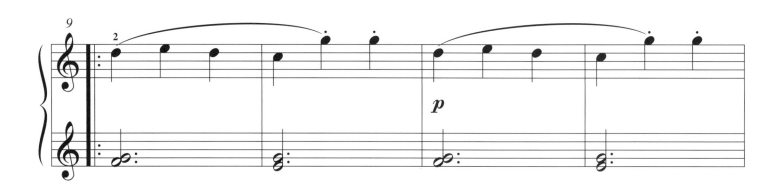

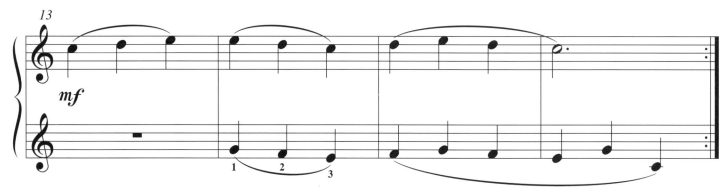

# ETUDE

*(Opus 101, Nos. 70 and 71)*

- Keep the melody singing beautifully, while the other hand supports it.

Ferdinand Beyer
(1803-1863)

**No. 70 Andante**

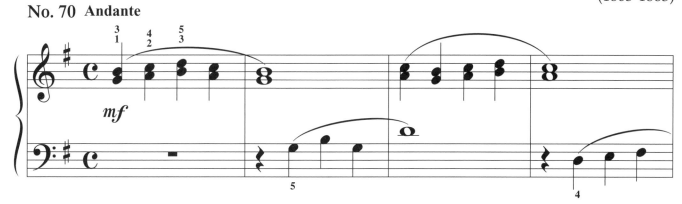

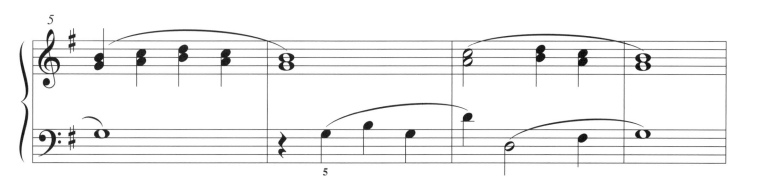

**No. 71**

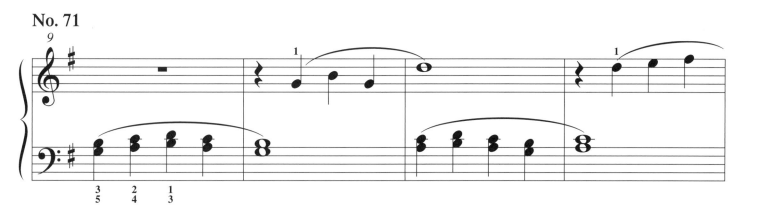

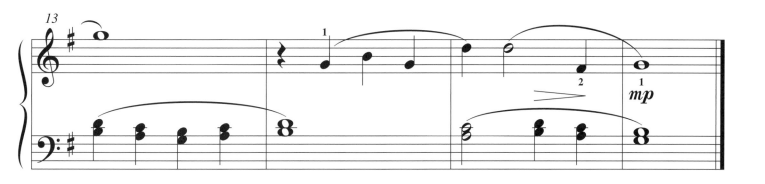

# THIS GREAT LAND

- Prepare the correct fingers over the correct keys *before* you play each beat. Remember, *never* reach for a key.

Valerie Roth Roubos
(1955-    )

**Majestically (♩ = ca. 112-120)**

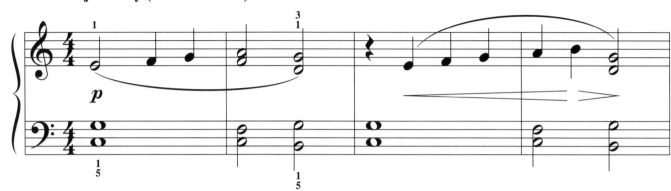

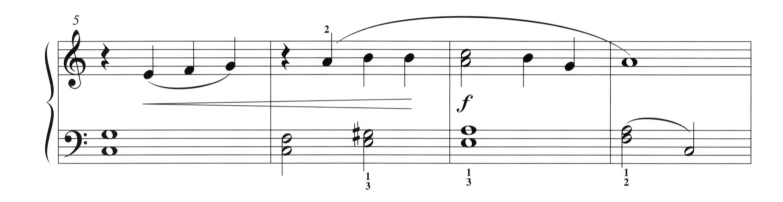

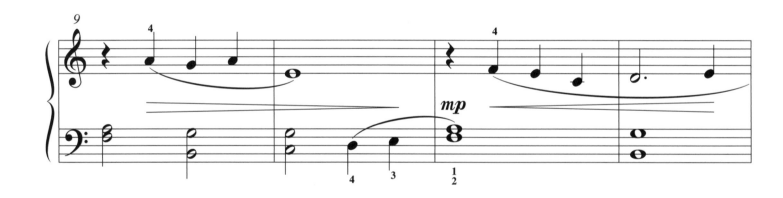

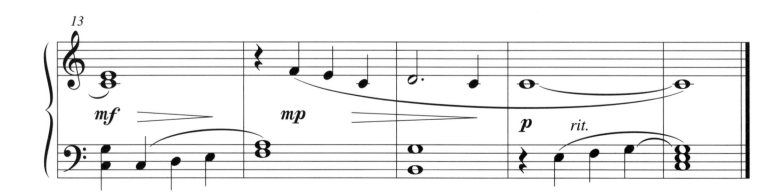

# ETUDE

## *(Opus 823, No. 18)*

• Before playing, label the harmonic intervals in the left hand.

Carl Czerny
(1791-1857)

# PRAYER

## *(Opus 107, No. 3)*

• Prepare every interval *before* playing it by resting your
fingers silently over the keys.

Carl Reinecke
(1824-1910)

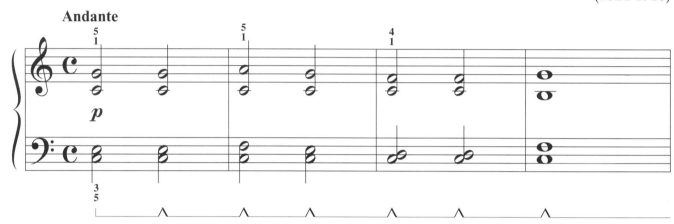

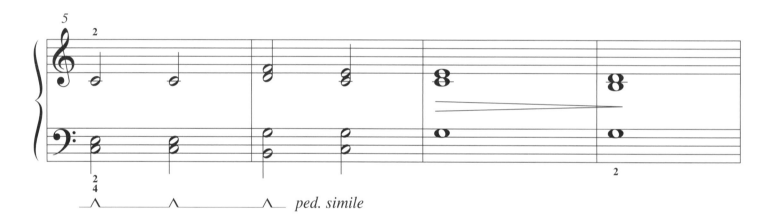

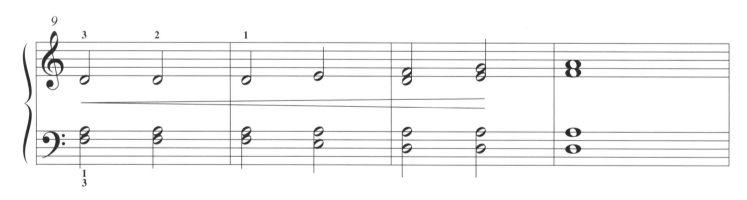

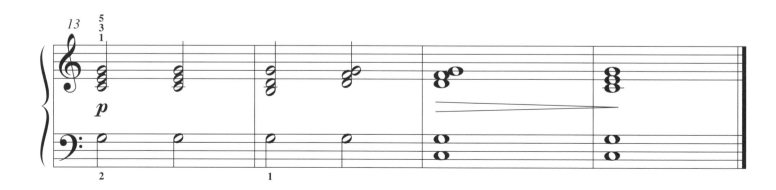

# SONG OF THE MOUNTAIN

• Play the left hand gently and smoothly, with expressive
shaping of the right-hand melody.

Robert Schultz
(1948-    )

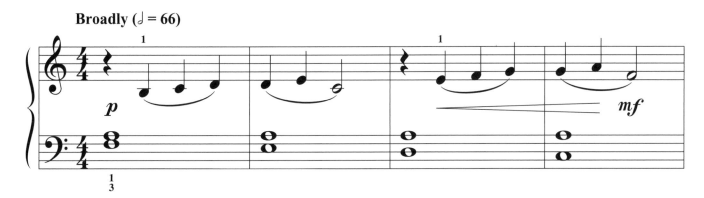

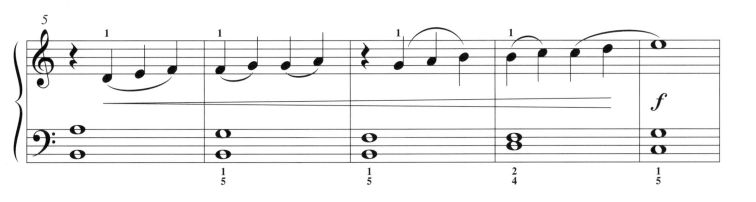

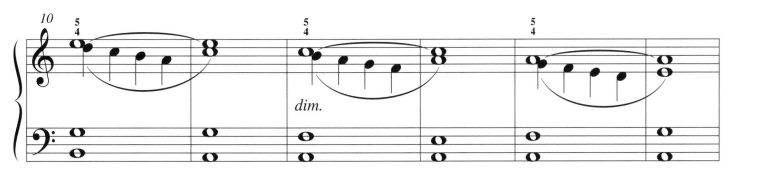

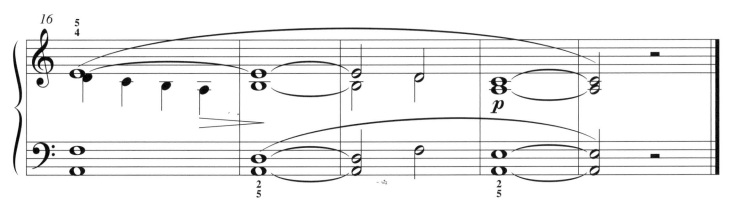

# ABOUT THE PIECES AND THE COMPOSERS

## Unit 1 - Five-Finger Patterns

**Etude**, *Op. 101, No. 15* by Ferdinand Beyer (1803-1863)
Ferdinand Beyer's *Elementary Instruction Book for the Pianoforte,* Op. 101, has become one of the most popular books for learning to play the instrument. Although originally published during his lifetime, it has continued to be used to the present day. Both hands remain in the same position for this piece, and the quick motion of one hand is always balanced by longer tones in the other hand, making it easier to learn.

**Etude**, *Op. 70, No. 10* by Hermann Berens (1826-1880)
(Johann) Hermann Berens was born in Germany and first studied music with his father, a famous flute player. He was active as a music director at several theaters, and later was a professor of composition at the Swedish Royal Academy. In addition to his work as an opera director, he also taught piano to nobility, including the queen of Sweden. In playing this piece, you might find it helps to notice that even though the hands often seem to be going in different directions, the similar direction from beat three in each measure to the downbeat of the next measure keeps them working together.

**Woodland Elves**, by Valerie Roth Roubos (b. 1955)
Valerie Roth Roubos earned degrees in music theory, composition, and flute performance from the University of Wyoming. Ms. Roubos maintains a studio in her home in Spokane, Washington, where she teaches flute, piano, and composition. Her teaching philosophy and compositions reflect her belief that all students, from elementary to advanced, are capable of musical playing that incorporates sensitivity and expression. This piece is a good example of imitation, with the left hand repeating what the right hand plays for most of the etude. Release your wrist at the end of each phrase to be able to play with agility and delicacy.

**Etude**, *Op. 823, No. 12* by Carl Czerny (1791-1857)
Born in Vienna, Czerny is connected with two very famous musicians—he was a student of Beethoven and teacher of Franz Liszt. He started teaching at the age of fifteen, and began a long career of composing etudes for his many students, writing over 800 sets of pieces. This piece requires careful attention to the notes of both hands, as you will find that they often move in the same direction but with different intervals.

**The Great Gate of Kazan**, by Timothy Brown (b. 1959)
The Great Kazan or "Kettle" is a narrow gorge located close to the legendary bridge erected by Apollodorus of Damascus in ancient times. The great "Iron Gate" on the Danube River now serves as a separation point between Serbia and Romania. Kazan, or *Tatar*, is the modern day capital city of the Republic of Tatarstan. While playing this etude, aim for a full tone and big contrasts of dynamics to give the impression of a majestic procession. As you look through the piece, you will notice the hands play in unison with full song-like phrasing.

## Unit 2 - Staccato

**Etude**, *Op. 82, No. 19* by Cornelius Gurlitt (1820-1901)
Only the right hand plays *staccato* in this piece by Gurlitt, a well-known teacher of the Romantic era, and a composer of many teaching etudes. Make the *staccato* notes light and soft for a perfect accompaniment to the singing left-hand melody. If you start with your fingertips on the keys and spring up by pushing off, you will have a beautiful tone and crisp *staccato*.

**Allegro**, from *24 Short and Easy Pieces, Op. 1* by Alexander Reinagle (1756-1809)
Born and educated in Scotland, Alexander Reinagle moved to the newly-formed United States of America in 1786 to settle in Philadelphia. He was a leader in introducing the music of Mozart and Haydn to the people of Philadelphia, and was a friend of the George Washington family, as well as a teacher of Washington's adopted daughter. Listen for a clear contrast between the smooth phrases and *staccato* notes of this piece, keeping the character very dance-like.

**Etude**, from *24 Five-Finger Exercises, Op. 777, No. 3* by Carl Czerny (1791-1857)
Czerny was an important link to many of the composers of the Classical and Romantic eras, passing traditions on to several famous students. He was the first to use the word "etude" for a piece dedicated to one technical or musical concept, and composed over 800 collections of them for teaching such famous students as Beethoven's nephew and Franz Liszt. To make the right-hand notes smooth while playing the crisp left-hand *staccato* needed for this piece, try "stop practice" in which you stop as soon as you have played the *staccato* to listen for the held right-hand note ready to play smoothly to the next note.

**Stop at Nothing**, by Timothy Brown (b. 1959)
This fun piece will give you lots of practice in playing crisp *staccato* in both hands as well as *tenuto* in the left hand. Start by playing hands separately until you are comfortable with the chords and the notes. Listen carefully so your left-hand chords that have *tenuto* come off the keys exactly when the right hand plays the second beat. Be sure to end each phrase with crisp notes, and "stop at nothing" until you can!

**Etude**, *Op. 823, No. 11* by Carl Czerny (1791-1857)
In order to learn this piece quickly and easily, play the left hand alone until you can play the chords by feel only. Then if you block the notes of the right hand by playing together every note that would be played in each measure, you will find them easy to read. Enjoy the dance-like feel of this playful piece by stressing the first beat and making the last three quarter notes of each measure light and crisp.

# Unit 3 - Legato

**Etude**, *Op. 101, No. 39* by Ferdinand Beyer (1803-1863)
Listen for a singing melody as you play with connected fingers and a rested arm (relaxed arm weight) supported by your fingers. To help in reading the notes, block the left hand in groups of two notes, first alone and then blocked while playing the right hand. Notice that if you didn't play the repeating D of the left hand, the moving notes of both hands would be a duet in similar directions. A fluent reader is able to use patterns such as these to get the notes learned quickly and move on to the fun of listening for a smooth, singing tone.

**Etude**, *Op. 190, No. 16* by Louis Köhler (1820-1886)
Louis Köhler was an important teacher and composer of the Romantic era, and an influence on Franz Liszt and Richard Wagner through his work as a writer. In addition to many collections of piano etudes, he also composed three operas, a ballet, and was a music critic as well as a leader in forming an important group of Romantic composers. You will find this piece much easier to learn if you leave out the G of the left hand and play only the notes that move with the right hand. Instead of many notes to learn, it is just a duet of right and left hand with a soft repeating note.

**Ice Crystals**, by Valerie Roth Roubos (b. 1955)
Bring out the top note in each harmonic third interval by emphasizing it more loudly than the lower note. Listen for a delicate left hand by moving your wrist and arm in a clockwise motion throughout.

**Etude**, *Op. 190, No. 22* by Louis Köhler (1820-1886)
After studying in Vienna, Louis Köhler took a position in Konigsberg, a part of Germany that is now called Kaliningrad in Lithuania. Listen for a rich, singing tone in the left hand as you connect the notes by being sure a finger rests on the key at all times. "Walk" your fingers from key to key, letting each roll to the next one. If you imagine the smooth glide of a slippery snake and keep your fingers gently curved, you will hear a beautiful, smooth melody.

**Etude**, by François Couperin (1668-1733)
Known as "Couperin the Great" to tell him apart from other members of his musically talented family, François Couperin lived in Paris and served as Court Organist for the Royal Chapel of Louis the XIV. His many harpsichord pieces were grouped into "orders" rather than the more traditional dances of the suite. Notice that the first measure of this piece is incomplete, and that the eighth notes are upbeats to the stronger downbeat of each measure. You can make the shifts to new notes easier by moving your fingers in a rolling motion to the top finger of your hands as you play up the scales.

# Unit 4 - Two-Note Slurs

**Etude**, *Op. 117, No. 10* by Cornelius Gurlitt (1820-1901)
Each two-note slur found in this piece needs the gentle land and wrist roll that you have practiced in the previous etudes. You should hear a very clear difference between the tone of the first note and the softer second one. Be careful to check the fingering of the left hand—if you play the correct fingering, it makes the two-note slurs in that hand very natural to play, and the legato with both notes very smooth.

**Der Dudelsack**, *Op. 95, No. 1* by Heinrich Kaspar Schmid (1874-1953)
A native of Regensburg, Germany, Schmid studied music at the Munich Academy of Music. He was a Professor of Music in Munich, at Karlsruhe Conservatory, and Augsburg, before starting a career as an independent composer in an area close to Munich. This piece is called a "musette" which would have been played by a bagpipe. The open fifths of the left hand sound like the steady drone of the bagpipe, while the right hand has a dance-like melody. Be sure to make the second note of the two-note slur short, rather than connecting it to the next detached note!

**Two by Two**, by Robert Schultz (b. 1948)
Since 1980, the name Robert Schultz has represented a standard of excellence for piano compositions and arrangements. His more than 500 publications from the world's leading publishers cover the range of original piano works, popular music, and classical editions, at all levels from beginning through professional. In this study, the hands stay within a five-finger position, but shift in a descending pattern every measure. If you look at the patterns of two-notes slurs before playing the piece, you will be able to plan where your hands will move.

# Unit 5 - Two-Part Counterpoint

**Etude**, *Op. 117, No. 4* by Cornelius Gurlitt (1820-1901)
This etude is from a collection by Gurlitt called *First Steps of the Young Pianist* and was one of the first pieces for the training of independence between the hands. Notice that even though you won't be playing the same notes in each

hand, there are many similarities, either in parallel or contrary (mirrored) motion. During the second beat of each half note, and before moving to each note, think of how the hands relate and the direction you will need to move.

**Canon No. 15**, from *200 Canons, Op. 14* by Konrad Max Kunz (1812-1875)
Born in a city in Bavaria, Germany, Konrad Kunz is best known as the composer of the Bavarian national hymn. The 200 canons he composed for piano are studies in using the hands independently. Both hands play the same D minor pattern throughout. Let the *staccato* notes followed by the accented notes help you to keep this piece steady.

**Study in Contrary Motion**, by Johann Friedrich Reichardt (1752-1814)
This composer led an interesting life, combining his interest in politics and the French Revolution with his work in music. Although he worked as a government official, his ability as a piano virtuoso led him to work for the Royal Prussian Court, and later for the brother of Napoleon. He was a close friend of many of the greatest poets and writers of the Romantic era, and his over 1500 songs were composed about the same time as those of Schubert. This study in contrary motion is a clever use of counterpoint in which the independence of the hands is simply a mirror of the other hand.

**Duo**, by Tomás de Santa Maria (ca.1510-1570)
A Spanish organist, composer, and music theorist of early music, Tomás de Santa Maria wrote a book on how to improvise in counterpoint. His work was very influential in the late Baroque era, and this piece is an excellent example of the independence of hands that would be expected in this style. If you have learned the notes and fingerings very well, you may want to try this with your teacher or a friend before putting both hands together. Notice that the first notes of the right hand are in bass clef!

**Etude**, *Op. 82, No. 17* by Cornelius Gurlitt (1820-1901)
Just as in the previous canons, the melody found in one hand is echoed later by the other hand. Be sure to mark the ends of phrases so you can lift one hand while the other continues! As in all counterpoint, noticing the parallel and contrary motion makes it possible to coordinate the two lines.

# Unit 6 - Harmonic Intervals

**Etude**, *Op. 101, No. 18* by Ferdinand Beyer (1803-1863)
Most of the left-hand accompaniment for this piece is made up of harmonic intervals, but when you play individual notes, you should look for the parallel motion of lines. Be sure you check the clef signs before you start since both hands are to be played above Middle C!

**Etudes**, *Op. 101, Nos. 70* and *71* by Ferdinand Beyer (1803-1863)
These two pieces are a pair of etudes composed by Beyer to work with the interval of a 3rd. To get the intervals to sound precisely together, you will need to move the hand directly above the new third, and then drop into the key bottom with firm but not stiff fingers. Notice the important moves of each hand, so prepare these in the quarter rests ahead of them.

**This Great Land**, by Valerie Roth Roubos (b. 1955)
Practice hands separately so the intervals are easy to play. When practicing hands together, focus on complete accuracy by preparing the correct fingers over the correct keys before playing each interval.

**Etude**, *Op. 823, No. 18* by Carl Czerny (1791-1857)
This etude has many shifts of five-finger patterns and some harmonic intervals larger than a 5th, making separate-hands practice a good idea. It is also a piece that would benefit from chain linking practice, in which two-measure groups that are well-learned are linked to the ones before and after them. Keep the repeated notes a light *staccato* for a dance-like feel.

**Prayer**, *Op. 107, No. 3* by Carl Reinecke (1824-1910)
Born in Denmark, Carl Reinecke was an important teacher and composer. He taught at the Leipzig Conservatory where his students included many famous Romantic composers. He held the post of director of the Gewandhaus Orchestra, an important position. When he was 80 years old, he made a recording of his playing on a piano roll, making him the first pianist to have been recorded. In playing this piece, as in playing any four-part harmony, look for the notes that change and the ones that stay the same from chord to chord. If you can play the harmonic intervals by feel, you will be very secure when playing hands together.

**Song of the Mountain**, by Robert Schultz (b. 1948)
This is a study in intervals—harmonic intervals in the left hand, and harmonic intervals in the right hand in the last half of the piece. Practice the harmonic intervals in the left hand first, and then block the downbeats of every measure, hands together, in measures 10-20. Notice that you will progress through intervals from a 3rd to a 7th on the white keys. Lastly, plan the rhythmic patterns in the first half of the piece and you'll be ready to play!